FOOTBALL

BY BRIAN HOWELL

CONTENT CONSULTANT
BARRY WILNER
ASSOCIATED PRESS NATIONAL FOOTBALL REPORTER

Published by ABDO Publishing Company, PO Box 398166, Minneapolis, MN 55439. Copyright ©
2012 by Abdo Consulting Group, Inc. International copyrights reserved in all countries. No part of
this book may be reproduced in any form without written permission from the publisher. SportsZone™
is a trademark and logo of ABDO Publishing Company.

Printed in the United States of America,
North Mankato, Minnesota
102011
012012

 THIS BOOK CONTAINS AT LEAST 10% RECYCLED MATERIALS.

Editor: Chrös McDougall
Copy Editor: Anna Comstock
Series Design and Cover Production: Craig Hinton
Interior Production: Kelsey Oseid

Photo Credits: Stephan Savoia/AP Images, cover (bottom); Craig Barhorst/iStockphoto, cover (top);
AP Images, 1, 13, 14, 19, 25, 29, 31, 34, 58 (bottom); Paul Jasienski/AP Images, 5; Dave Martin/
AP Images, 8; Mark Humphrey/AP Images, 10; Pro Football Hall of Fame/AP Images, 21, 58 (top);
NFL Photos/AP Images, 22, 37, 38, 58 (middle), 59 (top), 59 (middle); Raul Demolina/AP Images,
41; Greg Trott/AP Images, 44; John Raoux/AP Images, 47; John Russell/AP Images, 49; Smiley N.
Pool/Houston Chronicle/AP Images, 51; Matt York/AP Images, 55, 59 (bottom); Charles Krupa/AP
Images, 56

Library of Congress Cataloging-in-Publication Data
Howell, Brian, 1974-
  Football / by Brian Howell.
    p. cm. -- (Best sport ever)
  Includes index.
  ISBN 978-1-61783-142-3
  1. Football--Juvenile literature. I. Title.
  GV950.7.H69 2012
  796.332--dc23
                         2011034600

TABLE of CONTENTS

MAY 1 7 2012

CHAPTER 1

THE SUPER BOWL

Terrible Towels and Cheeseheads filled Cowboys Stadium in Arlington, Texas. Millions of fans gathered around television sets all across the world. On this February night, the Pittsburgh Steelers and the Green Bay Packers were playing for the ultimate prize in football—the Vince Lombardi Trophy.

Each year, the Super Bowl features the two best teams in the National Football League (NFL). On February 6, 2011, Super Bowl XLV also hosted two of the most storied teams in the history of the game.

The Packers represent the NFL's beginnings. The team began in 1919. Then it joined the NFL in 1921. That was only the second season of NFL football. Many early NFL teams were from

The Green Bay Packers and the Pittsburgh Steelers faced off in Super Bowl XLV. They are two of the NFL's most storied teams.

smaller cities such as Green Bay. As the NFL grew, many of those teams folded or moved to bigger cities. The Packers were the one exception. In 2011, Green Bay remained the smallest city to have its own NFL team.

Packers fans have much pride in their team. In fact, Packers fans are the only ones in the NFL who actually own their team. They come from all over Wisconsin to support the Packers on Sunday. Wisconsin is known as "America's Dairyland." So Packers fans have long worn the large foam cheese pieces on their heads to support their team.

"It's a college-like atmosphere in Green Bay," Packers quarterback Aaron Rodgers said. "Everywhere you go you see green and gold, it's a first-name basis [between the fans and players], and there's just a special connection that's always been there between the players and the fans."

THE NFL

The Houston Texans joined the NFL in 2002. That gave the league an even 32 teams. NFL teams are split between the American Football Conference (AFC) and the National Football Conference (NFC). Each conference has four, four-team divisions. As of Super Bowl XLV, all but four active NFL teams have experienced a Super Bowl at least once. Only the Cleveland Browns, the Detroit Lions, the Houston Texans, and the Jacksonville Jaguars had not.

The Packers have also been the most successful team in NFL history. They had already won 12 league titles going into Super Bowl XLV. That was more than any team. Nine of those championships came before the creation of the Super Bowl in 1967. Back then, the league champion was determined by regular-season record or a final game known as the NFL Championship Game.

Green Bay's history and success make the team special to its fans. The team is also very important to the league. In fact, the Super Bowl trophy itself is named after legendary Packers coach Vince Lombardi. At Super Bowl XLV, the Packers hoped to once again bring home the Lombardi Trophy. But it would not be easy.

LOMBARDI'S MARK

Vince Lombardi became a head coach in 1959. He lasted just nine years with the Green Bay Packers and then one with the Washington Redskins. But Lombardi never had a losing record. He also led the Packers to five NFL titles and to two Super Bowl victories. Lombardi died of cancer at age 57 on September 3, 1970. Many consider him to be the best NFL coach ever.

Paul Brown was another legendary NFL coach. He founded the Cleveland Browns in 1946 and coached them to 158 wins and seven league titles in 17 years. He also founded the Cincinnati Bengals in 1968 and coached them to 55 wins in eight seasons.

George Halas won 318 games and six league championships in 40 years with the Chicago Bears, beginning in 1920. Curly Lambeau founded the Packers in 1919 and coached them to 226 wins and six NFL titles during their first 33 NFL seasons. Tom Landry guided the Dallas Cowboys from 1960 to 1988. He won 250 games and two Super Bowls.

Pittsburgh Steelers fans wave their Terrible Towels to support their team at Super Bowl XLV.

The Steelers have been a part of the NFL since 1933. Through 2011, only the Steelers and the Dallas Cowboys had played in eight Super Bowls. But no team could match the six Super Bowl trophies the Steelers had won. The Steelers' tough, physical style of play attracts many fans to root for them. And one way fans root for the team is by waving their yellow Terrible Towels at Steelers games.

"Obviously you see them everywhere we go," Steelers quarterback Ben Roethlisberger said of Pittsburgh fans before the Super Bowl. "I always say that Pittsburgh fans are the best fans in all of sport. I think that's what this game, why it's going to be so awesome because Packer fans, I know they travel and I know their passion about their Packers. That's why I think this is the ultimate game and the ultimate two teams playing in it."

Game Time

The Super Bowl is the ultimate game for many sports fans. Football has established itself as the most popular sport in the United States. And the Super Bowl is its biggest game. More than 100,000 people filled Cowboys Stadium for Super Bowl XLV. Millions more watched on TV. In fact, roughly 162.9 million people tuned in. That made it the most-watched TV program in US history.

NFL players are among the most recognizable athletes in the United States. Many are paid millions of dollars each year just to play. And many of the stadiums they play in are extraordinary.

WHY THE NAME?

The Green Bay Packers got their nickname from a packing company that sponsored the team in 1919. The Pittsburgh Steelers are named for the city's heritage in the steel industry. Several other NFL teams are named for the heritage of their city or state, as well. Among them are the Minnesota Vikings (named for the Nordic roots of many people in the northern Midwest), the New England Patriots (named for the founding fathers of the United States), and the San Francisco 49ers (named after the California Gold Rush in 1849).

Packers quarterback Aaron Rodgers holds the Lombardi Trophy after leading his team to victory in Super Bowl XLV.

Super Bowl XLV was held in Cowboys Stadium. It had only opened just two years earlier, in 2009. The stadium had cost more than $1 billion to build.

Cowboys Stadium made history that night. Green Bay defeated Pittsburgh 31–25. That gave the Packers their 13th league championship and fourth Super Bowl title.

Super Bowl XLV also showed how much had changed over the years. Football in 2011 is nothing like it was at its beginning in the 1800s. Much had even changed since the NFL was formed in 1920. In those days, players wore leather helmets and played in front of small crowds. Most held regular jobs outside of football to help pay their bills. Today, football—at the high school, college, and professional level—has become one of the most popular forms of entertainment in the United States.

CHAPTER 2

THE EARLY DAYS

Rutgers University and Princeton University had an intense rivalry. After all, the two schools are located just 20 miles (32.19 km) apart in New Jersey. In 1869, Rutgers and Princeton played each other in a baseball game. Princeton won easily, 40–2.

Rutgers sought revenge for that loss. So the school challenged Princeton in football. At the time, football looked more like rugby and soccer than the football we know today. Those two games were growing in popularity throughout Europe.

However, the rules were not standardized yet. Rutgers captain William J. Leggett and Princeton captain William Gunmere agreed to follow the rules of the London Football Association for their game.

The Yale Bulldogs were often among the nation's best college football teams during the late 1800s.

Walter Camp coached Yale and then Stanford from 1888 to 1895. He had an 81–5–3 career record.

The two squads were set to play three games. The first came on November 6, 1869, at Rutgers. Each team played with 25 players. They used a round ball. Players were only allowed to kick or bat the ball with their feet, hands, heads, or sides. To score, a team would have to kick or bat the ball over the goal line. Each goal was worth one point.

Rutgers won 6–4. With that, college football was born. Princeton won the second game 8–0 one week later. The third game was canceled. Faculty members complained that the games interfered with the students' study time.

During the next decade, several colleges began fielding teams. Many of them were on the East Coast. Many of the earliest teams were from the prestigious Ivy League. Among them were Columbia, Harvard, Pennsylvania, and Yale.

Father of Football

Walter Camp is often referred to as "The Father of American Football." He played a major role in shaping the game of football into what it is today.

Camp was a star player for Yale from 1877 to 1882. He is credited with creating many key rules of the game. Camp came up with 11-man teams. He invented the play from scrimmage, where the center snaps the ball. He developed the system in which teams must gain 10 yards within four downs. Camp also developed a scoring system in which touchdowns were worth more points than kicks. Meanwhile, two points could be awarded for tackling an opponent in their own end zone.

Camp was on the American Football Rules Committee until he died in 1925. He also helped develop the National Collegiate Athletic Association (NCAA). That organization governs college sports. And, it was Camp who selected the first All-America team in college football in 1889.

Football was mostly a running game in the early days. Camp was one of the first people to recognize the importance of the quarterback. In addition, Camp authored several books about the sport. Several men helped develop modern football, but Camp might have been the most influential.

CARLISLE DOMINATES

Ivy League schools dominated college football in the early days. But the best team might have been the Carlisle Indian Industrial School in Pennsylvania. The Carlisle Indians are credited with pioneering the use of the forward pass and using trick plays. Led by legendary football figures Jim Thorpe and coach Glenn Scobey "Pop" Warner, the Indians dominated. Perhaps the greatest game Carlisle ever played came on November 9, 1912. Thorpe and Warner led the Indians to a 27–6 win over Army. Future US President Dwight Eisenhower was a player for Army in that game. Carlisle closed in 1918.

Other Football Leaders

John Heisman had been a college player and college coach. He played a major role in getting the forward pass legalized. However, most people today know him for the Heisman Memorial Trophy. It is given out to the top college football player each season.

Heisman was the first athletic director of the Downtown Athletic Club (DAC) in New York City. While there, he helped organize an award given to the best college football player each season. The award became known as the DAC trophy. The first one was awarded to University of Chicago halfback Jay Berwanger in 1935. Heisman died soon after. In 1936, the trophy was renamed to honor Heisman. It has been an annual part of college football ever since.

Amos Alonzo Stagg was another football innovator. He was a star player for Yale. In fact, he was on the first All-America team in 1889. Stagg also coached for more than 40 years. He is credited with many innovations in the game. Among them was sending players in motion on offense. Stagg also introduced numbers on player uniforms and began the tradition of awarding varsity letters in college.

When people hear the name Pop Warner today, most think of youth football leagues around the United States. Those leagues are part of the Pop Warner Little Scholars organization. It is named after one of its founders, Glenn Scobey "Pop" Warner.

Warner's legacy is much deeper than that, though. He was also a great football coach and innovator during his time. Warner coached from 1895 to 1939. He introduced the use of shoulder and thigh pads. He also brought to the game the spiral punt, the spiral pass, the three-point stance, and several formations still used today.

The Game Grows

It took some time for football to develop into the game we know today. Blocking and tackling were not part of the game when Rutgers and Princeton first suited up. But they became basic football fundamentals during the late 1800s. There was very little

HOMECOMING

One of the great traditions in high schools and colleges is homecoming. That is when alumni return to a school for a football game. In addition to a football game, many schools also have parades, pep rallies, and other events to celebrate the occasion. Many different schools claim to have invented homecoming. However, the University of Missouri is widely credited with having the first one in 1911. That year, Missouri's athletic director called alumni back to cheer on the Tigers in a game against the archrival Kansas Jayhawks. The celebration included pep rallies, a parade, a bonfire, and—of course—a football game. However, the game ended in a 3–3 tie.

Glenn Scobey "Pop" Warner's youth football league began with just four teams in 1923. In 2011, more than 5,000 teams were playing.

equipment in the early years. Helmets and shoulder pads were a long way from being introduced. The ball was just about the only piece of equipment used.

Despite the rule changes, football grew in popularity. By 1889, colleges all around the country fielded football teams. The sport spread from the Ivy League schools in the east to Southern California schools out west. There were 27 recognized college football teams in 1889. Ten years later, there were 73. That number would only grow in the following years.

CHAPTER 3

GOING PRO

W illiam "Pudge" Heffelfinger suited up for the Allegheny Athletic Association on November 12, 1892. He played well, too. He returned a fumble for the game's only points in a 4–0 win over the Pittsburgh Athletic Club. A touchdown was worth four points at the time.

It was no surprise to see Heffelfinger play well. After all, he had been a great player at Yale. He was a member of the first All-America team in 1889. And he was the first three-time All-American. That was not what made him unique on this day, however. What set him apart was the $500 he was paid to play. It was the only game Heffelfinger played professionally. But he is known as the first professional football player.

In today's dollars, William "Pudge" Heffelfinger was paid approximately $12,000 for one game. The NFL minimum in 2010 was $20,000 per game.

Jim Thorpe of the Canton Bulldogs leaps with the ball during a 1915 game against the Columbus Panhandles. Both teams later played in the NFL.

Professional football soon took off. Clubs began to openly pay players. Allegheny fielded the first team of all professionals in 1896. They only played together for two games. But other clubs throughout small towns in the United States soon followed. They played full seasons with professionals.

The game lacked organization at the professional level, however. Businessman Joe Carr wanted to change that. He set up a meeting on September 17, 1920, in Canton, Ohio. Many of the game's great innovators attended. Among them were George

Halas, Curly Lambeau, and Jim Thorpe. At that meeting, the American Professional Football Association (APFA) was formed. Two years later, the league changed its name to the NFL.

Influential Figures

Carr served as the president of the NFL from 1921 to 1939. He gave the league the stability it needed. He established player contracts. That prevented players from jumping from team to team. He was also influential in creating a schedule system, a championship game, and a college draft.

Halas founded the Decatur Staleys. That team later became the Chicago Bears. There was another Chicago team that played in the 1920 APFA season. It was known as the Cardinals. Today the Cardinals play in Arizona. The Bears and the Cardinals are the only active NFL teams who played in that first 1920 AFPA season.

Halas played for the Bears. He also coached them for 40 years. He led the team to six NFL titles. In addition, Halas was responsible for several league rules that are still in place. One example is the forward pass being legal from anywhere behind the line of scrimmage. Halas and Carr also played a big role in creating the NFL Championship Game, which began in 1933.

Lambeau founded the Green Bay Packers in 1919. He spent 31 years coaching the Packers. He became the first coach in professional football to run a pass-first offense. Lambeau proved that teams could win by throwing the ball.

Thorpe was named the first president of the APFA. However, he handed the position to Carr after just one year. Many consider Thorpe to be one of the greatest athletes of all time. He was a star in football and baseball. He also won two gold medals in track and field at the 1912 Olympic Games in Stockholm, Sweden.

GOING BOWLING

While professional football was gaining a foothold in the United States, college football was booming. From 1916 through 1933, the Rose Bowl was the only postseason bowl game that was played annually. In 1934, the Sugar Bowl and the Orange Bowl began. In 1965, there were nine bowl games firmly established. By 2011, there were 35. The Rose Bowl, known as "The granddaddy of them all," remains among the most prestigious.

Red Grange of Illinois returns the opening kickoff 95 yards for a touchdown against Michigan in 1924.

Tough Times

Even with an organized league, professional football struggled. Games were not yet broadcast on television or radio. Newspapers did not write much about the NFL, either. "The college game was what everyone cared about," Halas said.

The biggest college football star at the time was Red Grange. He was a halfback from the University of Illinois. Although just 5-foot-10 and 170 pounds, the "Galloping Ghost" was a three-time All-American. After one game, author Damon Runyon

THROWING THE BALL

NFL quarterbacks make throwing a football look easy. They drop back to pass and rocket perfect spirals to their receivers. But it takes practice to make the oblong ball travel through the air in a spiral. A quarterback must grip the ball a certain way. The quarterback also must have the proper release point so the ball goes where he wants it to go.

wrote, "This man Red Grange of Illinois is three or four men and a horse rolled into one."

NFL teams took notice. The Bears signed Grange to play for them. He played his first game for the Bears five days after helping Illinois beat Ohio State. Grange and the Bears took on the Chicago Cardinals at Cubs Field. The stadium is now known as Wrigley Field. Approximately 36,000 fans showed up for the game. That marked the largest number of fans to ever see a professional football game at that time.

The Bears wanted to promote their new star. Teams sometimes played several games each week at the time. But the Bears played 19 games in 66 days all around the country. That included eight games in a 12-day period. The Bears went to the Polo Grounds in New York on December 6, 1925. A whopping 73,000 fans attended the game between the Bears and the New York Giants. Grange was the star in Chicago's 19–7 win.

"Pro ball in the early days got two or three inches on the third page [of the newspaper]," Grange said. "After we made those tours, it was getting top headlines. We spread the NFL across the country."

Shining Stars

Grange proved that fans wanted to see great players. The NFL provided plenty of them. More and more fans began going to NFL games.

Other stars soon followed Grange in the NFL. Sammy Baugh, Otto Graham, Don Hutson, Sid Luckman, Bronko Nagurski, Ernie Nevers, and Steve Van Buren starred during the 1930s and 1940s. They helped the league grow greatly in popularity.

The NFL had great teams, too. The Bears and the Packers dominated the NFL. They won a combined 13 league titles from 1921 to 1946. The Detroit Lions,

BROWN STARS FOR BROWNS

Jim Brown joined the Cleveland Browns as a 21-year-old rookie in 1957. He is regarded as perhaps the greatest running back in NFL history. Brown led the league in rushing yards in eight of his nine seasons. He surprisingly retired after the 1965 season when he was only 29 years old. At the time of his retirement, Brown had 12,312 career rushing yards. That was more than 2,500 more than anyone else in pro football history at the time. He held the league rushing record until Walter Payton of the Chicago Bears broke the mark in 1984. As of 2011, Brown still ranked ninth in league history in rushing.

the Giants, and the Washington Redskins combined for another 10 titles from 1927 to 1957.

By the mid-1940s, professional football had become so popular that a second league formed. It was called the All-American Football Conference (AAFC). The league survived just four years, from 1946 to 1949. But it made a lasting impression on the sport. The AAFC's Cleveland Browns and San Francisco 49ers joined the NFL when the AAFC dissolved. The Browns had won all four AAFC titles. Both teams remain in the NFL today.

The NFL took another step forward in 1951. The Browns and the Los Angeles Rams played in that year's championship game. It was the first game to be televised across the country.

Behind a new crop of stars, the NFL was more popular than ever. Among the top players of the 1950s and 1960s were quarterbacks

THE GREATEST GAME

On December 28, 1958, the New York Giants and the Baltimore Colts met at Yankee Stadium in New York for the NFL title. There were 12 future Hall of Fame players on the field that day, including Colts quarterback Johnny Unitas. Three future Hall of Fame coaches were on the sideline. The game was one of the first professional football games to be televised nationally. It was also the first to go into sudden death overtime. Colts running back Alan Ameche ended the game with a one-yard touchdown run that gave Baltimore a 23–17 win. Many people consider it to be the greatest game of all time.

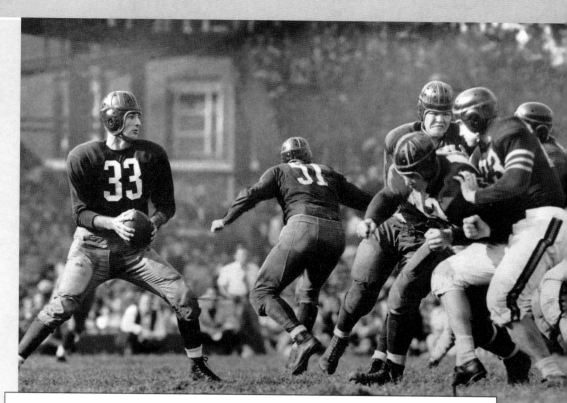

The Washington Redskins' Sammy Baugh threw 187 touchdowns, made 31 interceptions, and also punted during his 16 NFL seasons.

Bobby Layne, Y. A. Tittle, and Johnny Unitas; wide receivers Raymond Berry and Elroy "Crazylegs" Hirsch; running back Jim Brown; running back/receiver Frank Gifford; defensive back Dick "Night Train" Lane; and defensive end Gino Marchetti.

The Browns were often the top team during the 1950s. Quarterback Graham led the Browns to six straight league title games. They won three of them. However, the Browns' glory days would not carry into the next generation of pro football.

CHAPTER 4

A SUPER GAME

There was a popular toy during the 1960s called the Wham-O Superball. Whether or not that has a place in NFL history is not clear. But it is certainly part of football lore.

In 1960, the American Football League (AFL) formed as a rival to the NFL. Many viewed the AFL as a lesser league than the NFL. But the AFL proved to be a success. It featured many teams that are still in existence. It also featured some of professional football's top stars. Among them were wide receiver Lance Alworth, quarterback George Blanda, fullback Cookie Gilchrist, and quarterback Joe Namath.

The AFL and NFL were completely independent from 1960 to 1965. They played separate seasons and held separate

George Blanda, *left*, won the first two AFL championships with the Houston Oilers. He played for 26 seasons— a record still in 2011.

championship games. That began to change in 1966. Executives from both leagues began working together to develop a plan to merge the leagues. After the 1966 season, each league's winner would meet in a true championship game. Then, in 1970, they would officially merge together to form one, 26-team league.

The AFL-NFL merger proved to be one of the most important developments in professional football history. It also created football's most famous game. The AFL and NFL champions played against each other for the first time after the 1966 season. That's where the Wham-O Superball came into play.

Lamar Hunt was a founder of the AFL and the owner of the Kansas City Chiefs. At a 1966 owners meeting, Hunt first referred to the new championship game as the "Super Bowl." Hunt later figured he got the name from watching his kids play with their Wham-O Superballs.

ROZELLE TAKES OFFICE

Pete Rozelle was the 33-year-old general manager of the Los Angeles Rams in 1960. Some people were surprised that he was named NFL commissioner that year. However, Rozelle wound up serving as commissioner for 29 years. That was 12 years longer than anyone else in NFL history through 2011. Rozelle led the league through the development of the Super Bowl and the merger of the NFL and AFL. He also helped orchestrate huge television contracts and got the league through labor issues. Many consider Rozelle to be the architect of the NFL as we know it today. He died in 1996 at 70 years old.

MONDAY NIGHT FOOTBALL

NFL football has become synonymous with Sunday afternoons in the fall and early winter. In 1970, however, the league capitalized on an opportunity to play in front of a wider audience. That is when *Monday Night Football* was born. The NFL began showcasing one game per week in front of a national, prime-time audience. *Monday Night Football* has been a part of the NFL ever since.

Today, the 1966 championship game is known as Super Bowl I. However, it was known as the AFL-NFL World Championship Game when it was played. It was not until January 1970 that the game officially became known as the Super Bowl. That was the fourth playing of the game. But even throughout the 1966 season, the championship game was commonly referred to as the Super Bowl by fans and newspapers.

Super Bowl I

Fittingly, Hunt's Chiefs won the 1966 AFL title. That meant they would represent their league in Super Bowl I. They played the NFL champion Green Bay Packers on January 15, 1967. The game was held at Memorial Coliseum in Los Angeles. The event was hardly the spectacle that it is today. Just over 63,000 fans attended the game at the 92,000-seat stadium. CBS and NBC broadcast the game on television. Approximately 60

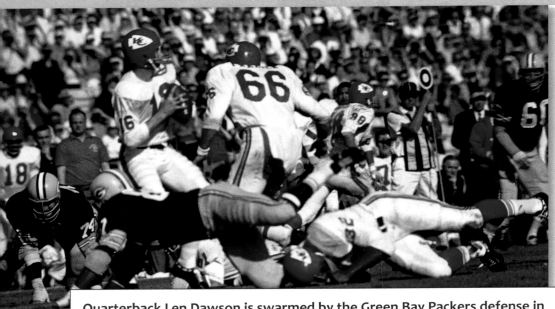

Quarterback Len Dawson is swarmed by the Green Bay Packers defense in a 35–10 loss in Super Bowl I.

million people in North America watched the game on television or listened on radio. But it was blacked out in the Los Angeles area. The Packers ultimately won the game 35–10. As the game became an annual event, the popularity of it increased. Super Bowl I was the only Super Bowl that was not a sellout. Every Super Bowl since then has been played in front of a full stadium.

AFL Success

Something else changed over the next few seasons: the AFL caught up to the NFL. The NFL's Packers won the first two Super

Bowls. They dominated the AFL champions both times. Green Bay had won five NFL titles during the 1960s. Legendary coach Vince Lombardi led a team that featured several Hall of Famers, including quarterback Bart Starr.

The Packers' dominance led many to believe that the NFL was the superior league. As such, few believed the NFL champion Baltimore Colts would have much trouble against the AFL champion New York Jets in Super Bowl III. Quarterback Joe Namath, from the AFL's New York Jets, disagreed.

He led the Jets into Super Bowl III against the heavily favored Colts. Before the game, Namath made a bold statement. "We're going to win Sunday," he said. "I'll guarantee you." He backed up his statement. Namath led the Jets to a shocking 16–7 win over the Colts. It was a big win for the Jets and for the AFL.

The AFL's Chiefs won Super Bowl IV in 1969. Then the two leagues merged into one for the 1970 season. The league kept the NFL name. With 26 teams, the NFL divided into two conferences. They were the National Football Conference (NFC) and American Football Conference (AFC). The AFC was made up of the former AFL teams, as well as three former NFL teams. Since the merger in 1970, the Super Bowl has featured the champions from the AFC and NFC.

Dynasties

The merger resulted in a strong, established NFL. The years that followed produced some of the greatest teams of all time. Among them was the Dallas Cowboys. Coach Tom Landry and Hall of Fame quarterback Roger Staubach led "America's Team." Behind Landry and Staubach, Dallas went to more Super Bowls (five) than anyone during the 1970s. The Cowboys won two of them.

The Minnesota Vikings dominated during the regular

COLLEGE POWERS

While professional football was booming, the college game was flourishing, as well. Several schools had established themselves as top programs. Nebraska, for example, had become a power program and won its first two national titles in 1970 and 1971. Notre Dame, Oklahoma, Southern California, and Alabama continued to dominate, as well. In addition to great teams, college football produced some of the greatest football players of all time during the 1970s. Earl Campbell, Tony Dorsett, Jack Ham, Mike Singletary, Lynn Swann, and Archie Griffin were some of the biggest stars in college football during those years.

Through 2011, Joe Namath was the only quarterback to win the Super Bowl Most Valuable Player Award without throwing a single touchdown.

seasons of the 1970s. From 1969 to 1976, they compiled a remarkable 87–24–1 record. Known as the "Purple People Eaters," Vikings defensive linemen Carl Eller, Gary Larsen, Jim Marshall, and Alan Page struck fear into opposing offenses. Quarterback Fran Tarkenton was not too shabby himself. Minnesota reached four Super Bowls during that time. However, the Vikings lost all four times.

The former AFL Miami Dolphins have made history on two accounts. They were the first team to reach the Super Bowl three

Through 2010, the 1972 Miami Dolphins remained the only team to go undefeated during the regular season and win the Super Bowl.

years in a row, from 1971 to 1973. In 1972, the Dolphins went undefeated throughout the regular season and the playoffs. They finished 17–0 and won the Super Bowl. Through 2011, no other team has matched that feat. Among the top Dolphins were Hall of Famers such as running back Larry Csonka and quarterback Bob Griese. Legendary coach Don Shula was at the helm. The Dolphins also won Super Bowl VIII following the 1973 season.

Although there were many strong teams during the 1970s, perhaps the strongest was the Pittsburgh Steelers. The Steelers won four Super Bowls during the decade. They were champions in 1974, 1975, 1978, and 1979. Twice, the Steelers defeated the Cowboys in the big game. The team had nine future Hall of Fame players during that time. Among them were quarterback Terry Bradshaw, running back Franco Harris, and defensive tackle "Mean" Joe Greene. Pittsburgh's legendary coach during that time, Chuck Noll, also went on to the Hall of Fame.

New NFL dynasties would emerge during the 1980s. However, the league would also struggle with off-field issues.

LEGENDARY LEADERS

Coaches are often the most recognizable men in college football. Paul "Bear" Bryant is one of the most legendary figures in college history. He won 232 games and six national championships at Alabama. He also coached at three other schools and retired with 323 total wins. Knute Rockne led Notre Dame to a 105–12–5 record and five national titles in 13 seasons before dying in a plane crash. Bobby Bowden (Florida State), Woody Hayes (Ohio State), Robert Neyland (Tennessee), Tom Osborne (Nebraska), Joe Paterno (Penn State), Eddie Robinson (Grambling), and Bud Wilkinson (Oklahoma) are all among the most respected college coaches.

Robinson coached Grambling for more than 55 years, winning a record 408 games. However, Paterno passed that record in 2011—his 46th and final season at Penn State—at age 84.

CHAPTER 5

FACING CHALLENGES

Few football fans will ever remember Ed Rubbert or Lionel Vital. But they both had a role in helping the Washington Redskins win the Super Bowl XXII in 1987.

NFL players went on strike over labor disagreements two games into the 1987 season. The NFL went one week without football. Then team owners found replacement players. Rubbert played quarterback and Vital played running back. For three weeks, they starred for the Redskins. They helped the team go 3–0 during the strike. The regular NFL players returned after that third game. Rubbert, Vital, and dozens of others like them never again played in the NFL.

The 1987 NFL players strike ended with the players returning to work after four weeks of striking and no concessions made by the owners.

The 1980s were an odd decade for football. On one hand, the sport had never been more popular. The NFL expanded to 28 teams in 1976 by adding the Seattle Seahawks and the Tampa Bay Buccaneers. The Super Bowl had also become the event of the year for many sports fans.

Dynamic players, great teams, and great tradition made college football as popular as ever. And at the high school level, more than 957,000 youth played football during 1979. That was an increase of approximately 55,000 from 1969.

Not all was well with the NFL, though. During the 1980s, the NFL shut down twice because of labor issues. The players went on strike during the 1982 season. That caused seven weeks of games to be wiped out. And the 1987 strike lasted four weeks.

The 1980s also saw three teams move. The Oakland Raiders went to Los Angeles in 1982. The Baltimore Colts went to Indianapolis in 1984. Then the St. Louis Cardinals went to Phoenix in 1988.

The NFL faced another challenge when a new league formed in 1983. It was called the United States Football League (USFL). The league lasted just three years. But it had a huge impact on the NFL. Some of the best college players went to the USFL instead of the NFL. Hall of Fame quarterbacks Jim Kelly and Steve Young both later led NFL teams to Super Bowls. But they got their starts in the USFL. With so much talent going to the USFL, player salaries in the NFL increased dramatically. That provided more strain on the owners.

Commissioner Pete Rozelle helped the NFL through all of that turmoil. And through it all, the league remained popular. Legendary players and great teams kept the fans in the stands, and the NFL thrived.

West Coast Offense

The San Francisco 49ers ruled the 1980s on the field. They went to four Super Bowls from 1981 to 1989. And they won them all. The 49ers' success was in large part due to their innovative head coach, Bill Walsh. His high-flying, pass-oriented offense became known as the West Coast Offense.

RUNNERS TAKE CENTER STAGE

The 1980s and 1990s featured many of the best running backs in NFL history. The Chicago Bears' Walter Payton retired after the 1987 season with a league-record 16,726 career yards. Barry Sanders of the Detroit Lions was well on his way to crushing that record when he abruptly retired after the 1998 season, at the age of 30. Sanders ranked second to Payton, with 15,269 yards, when he retired. Eric Dickerson (13,259 yards) and Tony Dorsett (12,739 yards) were also big-time stars during that era. But Emmitt Smith of the Dallas Cowboys would pass them all. He retired in 2004 after 15 seasons—the last two with the Arizona Cardinals—with a league-record 18,355 yards.

The San Francisco 49ers won three Super Bowls with coach Bill Walsh and quarterback Joe Montana running the West Coast Offense.

Many consider Joe Montana to be the greatest quarterback of all time. He led the 49ers to all four Super Bowl titles in the 1980s. He was named Super Bowl Most Valuable Player (MVP) three times. Beginning in 1985, the 49ers also had a player many believe to be the best wide receiver of all time in Jerry Rice. He played in San Francisco through 2000.

San Francisco's success did not end in the 1980s. Montana injured his elbow before the 1991 season and missed every game. But Young took over as quarterback and held the job through the 1998 season. The 49ers won at least 10 games in each of Young's seasons. He led them to a Super Bowl championship in 1994.

Other Stars

If not for Montana and the 49ers, Washington might have been the team of the 1980s. Coached by Joe Gibbs, the Redskins went to the Super Bowl three times in the 1980s. They won in both of the strike-shortened seasons, 1982 and 1987. Quarterback Joe Theismann and powerful Hall of Fame running back John Riggins led the team early in the decade. Three other Hall of Famers kept the Redskins among the elite teams throughout the 1980s and into the 1990s. They were cornerback Darrell Green, offensive lineman Russ Grimm, and receiver Art Monk. And quarterback Mark Rypien guided the Redskins to the Super Bowl crown in 1991.

Owner and general manager Al Davis has led the Oakland/Los Angeles Raiders since the 1960s. He has had multiple legal issues with the NFL. But Davis has guided a successful franchise.

SAN FRANCISCO TREAT

From 1985 to 2004, wide receiver Jerry Rice dominated like no receiver before him. As of 2011, he still held NFL records for catches (1,549), receiving yards (22,895), and touchdown catches (197)—and nobody else was even close. Rice played for San Francisco from 1985 to 2000 before ending his career with three-plus seasons with the Oakland Raiders and half a season with the Seattle Seahawks.

He was still at the helm in 2011. The Raiders reached five Super Bowls under Davis, winning three. They were never better than from 1980 to 1985. They went 61–28 and won two Super Bowls during that time.

The 1980s and 1990s were also great for the Denver Broncos. The Baltimore Colts selected star college quarterback John Elway in the 1983 draft. But Elway refused to sign with the Colts. So the team traded him to the Broncos. Elway then led the Broncos to five Super Bowls during his 16-year career. Elway and the Broncos lost their first three Super Bowls. However, they won back-to-back championships in 1997 and 1998.

From 1990 to 1993, the Buffalo Bills became the first, and only, team in NFL history to reach the Super Bowl four years in a row. Hall of Fame coach Marv Levy and quarterback Jim Kelly never led the Bills to a championship win, though.

University of Miami wide receiver Stanley Shakespeare catches a pass against the Nebraska Cornhuskers during the 1984 Orange Bowl.

Two of Buffalo's Super Bowl losses came against the Dallas Cowboys. Quarterback Troy Aikman, running back Emmitt Smith, and receiver Michael Irvin helped Dallas win three Super Bowls in four seasons from 1992 to 1995. Those three players became known as "The Triplets." All three were later enshrined in the Hall of Fame.

Changes around the League

Rozelle retired as commissioner in November 1989. Paul Tagliabue took over as the leader of the NFL. Tagliabue stayed in charge until 2006. His time as commissioner is widely viewed as a successful period for the NFL. Under Tagliabue, the league expanded from 28 to 32 teams. The league had a different geographical look by the end of the 1990s, though.

Los Angeles became an NFL city in 1946, when the Rams moved there from Cleveland. In 1994, the city had two teams—the Rams and the Raiders. But both teams moved after that season. The Raiders moved back to Oakland, and the Rams moved to St. Louis. Many attempts have been made to bring a team back to Los Angeles. However, the second largest city in the nation has not had an NFL team since 1994.

Cleveland had been home to pro football since 1937. But in 1996, Browns owner Art Modell moved his team to Baltimore. The city of Cleveland won a battle to keep the Browns logo and its history. So, Modell's team became known as the Baltimore Ravens. Cleveland went without a team

HUSKERS, SEMINOLES DOMINATE

From 1987 to 2000, coach Bobby Bowden's Florida State Seminoles won 152 games and lost just 19. They finished in the top five of the Associated Press rankings in each of those 14 years, including number one in 1993 and 1999. The Nebraska Cornhuskers also dominated during that time. The Cornhuskers have been one of the best programs in college football since the 1960s, and under coach Tom Osborne, the years from 1993 to 1997 were five of the most remarkable in school history. In those years, Nebraska went 60–3 and won three national titles. Nebraska won at least nine games every year from 1969 to 2001.

The Houston Texans and Tennessee Titans compete twice each year in the AFC South. Houston is the NFL's newest team, created in 2002.

for three years. Then in 1999, the NFL granted a new team to Cleveland. The Browns were back.

Houston briefly lost its team, too. The Houston Oilers were an original AFL team from 1960. But in 1997, they moved north to Tennessee. After two years as the Tennessee Oilers, they changed their name to the Titans in 1999. Houston got a new team in 2002 called the Texans. With the 1995 additions of the Carolina Panthers and the Jacksonville Jaguars, the Texans gave the NFL its current 32 teams.

POPULARITY SOARS

In many parts of the country, Friday nights in the fall mean one thing: high school football. Whether in big cities or rural communities, the glow of stadium lights brings people together every Friday night. High school football is a way of life in some states or small towns. During the 2009–10 school year, more than 15,000 high schools in the United States fielded football teams.

Some smaller communities do not have enough students to make up a full football team. They can still play high school football, though. Traditionally each team has 11 players at one time. But there are variations of the game in which six, eight, or nine players can be used. That allows smaller schools, which may only have 15 or 20 boys in the entire school, to play the game.

High school football brings communities together, big and small, across the United States during Friday nights in the fall.

No matter how many players are on the field, the game brings out a special passion in towns around the country. The teams represent the communities in which they play. In some states, such as Texas and Colorado, high school championship games are played in the same stadium where the local NFL team plays.

"I think of words like special and exciting when I think of Friday nights," said Ray Milavec, who broadcasts high school football games on WELW radio in Willoughby, Ohio. "I don't care if it is Game 1 or the playoffs. And I don't care if we are talking about a Mr. Football winner or the last kid on the bench. . . . It is a blessing that I get to stay involved with the kids at the high school level and with athletics on the area scene. There really is nothing like it."

Of course, the best high school players go on to play in college. There are several Web sites devoted to highlighting the top high school recruits in the country.

The Bowl Championship Series

Many sports leagues in the United States determine the champion through a playoff system. Division I college football is not one of them. Instead, it features a series of postseason bowl games. The bowl games allow teams that have a winning record to play one extra game. Each game features a match-up of two non-conference opponents with a similar record.

Reaching a bowl game is often the benchmark for a good season. However, the system has often left fans of the top teams unsatisfied. That is partly because the top two teams historically did not always play against each other. In the 56 seasons before 1992, the number one and number two teams met in the postseason just eight times.

Also, without a playoff system, there is often debate at the end of the season as to which team is the true champion. In 1990, for example, Associated Press voters

MUST-SEE TV

In 1936, the Philadelphia Eagles selected the University of Chicago's Jay Berwanger with the first pick in the first-ever NFL Draft. But the draft got little attention. For many years after that, it remained a relatively small event as well. The draft was simply designed for NFL teams to select the top college players.

All of that changed in 1980. That is when ESPN televised the entire draft and made it a big event. As of 2011, the seven rounds of the NFL Draft take place over three days, all of which are broadcast live on television. It has become a major event in the sports world.

named Colorado as the national champion. However, United Press International voters named Georgia Tech the champion. In 1991, Miami and Washington split the title.

Changes were made over the following years to improve the system. However, it was not until 1999 that the nation's two top-ranked teams were guaranteed to meet in a bowl game. That is when the Bowl Championship Series (BCS) began. Four of the most prestigious bowl games—the Fiesta Bowl, the Orange Bowl, the Sugar Bowl, and the Rose Bowl—make up the BCS. From 1999 to 2006, one of those games served as the national championship game. A separate BCS Championship Game was added in 2007. Every year, the top Division I teams strive to make a BCS bowl.

The system is not perfect. Various groups rank the top 25

OFFENSIVE STYLES

Over the years, football has evolved on the field. Coaches are always looking for better ways to defeat their opponents. During the early 2000s, the spread offense boomed in high school and college football. The spread offense features several receivers and lots of motion before the snap. It is also generally a fast-paced offense designed to score points quickly. Some of the best spread teams, including the University of Florida, rely on athletic quarterbacks who can beat teams by throwing or running the ball. Tim Tebow quarterbacked Florida's spread offense from 2006 to 2009. He is considered one of the greatest college players of all time. Facing bigger and faster talent in the NFL, spread quarterbacks are not as effective.

Boise State's Ian Johnson runs for the game-winning two-point conversion during the 2007 Fiesta Bowl against Oklahoma.

football teams each season. Sometimes they have different teams in the top two spots. Because of that, many still want to see a playoff system. However, with the BCS system in place, college football has generated more revenue than ever before.

Some college football powerhouse teams have found great success with the system as well. Among them are Florida, Louisiana State, Ohio State, Oklahoma, and Southern California.

Brady's Bunch Leads the Way

The New England Patriots were the class of the NFL during the early 2000s. Bill Belichick took over as the Patriots' head

Behind quarterback Tom Brady, the New England Patriots were a force in the early 2000s.

coach in 2000. The team finished 5–11. Then it started the 2001 season with two straight losses. That second loss looked even worse when starting quarterback Drew Bledsoe got hurt. Many considered Bledsoe to be the best quarterback in the team's history to that point.

Losing Bledsoe opened the door for little-known Tom Brady. He was a sixth-round pick in 2000. There were 198 players selected ahead of him. Nobody knew what to expect from Brady. But he won 11 of the 14 games he started in 2001. He then guided the Patriots to an upset of the St. Louis Rams in the Super Bowl. And through 2011, he has barely slowed down.

IRONMAN BRETT

In 1984, quarterback Ron Jaworski set an NFL record with 116 consecutive starts by a quarterback. Although still an impressive streak, Jaworski's mark was shattered by Brett Favre. From 1992 to 2010, Favre started in 297 straight games. He led the Packers to a victory in Super Bowl XXXI in 1997. Favre also played for the Atlanta Falcons, the Minnesota Vikings, and the New York Jets.

Through the 2010 season, Brady had led the Patriots to four Super Bowls. New England won three of them—in 2001, 2003, and 2004. In 2007, the Patriots joined the 1972 Miami Dolphins as the only teams in NFL history to go undefeated during the regular season. But unlike the Dolphins, the Patriots fell short in the Super Bowl. They lost to the New York Giants in Super Bowl XLII. So New England finished the season 18–1.

Football has many storied traditions that have lasted over the years. Whether it is high school games on Fridays, college games on Saturdays, or professional games on Sundays and Monday nights, people all around the United States passionately follow their teams. And although teams such as the Pittsburgh Steelers and the Green Bay Packers have won more championships than any of the other NFL teams, a common saying persists: "Any given Sunday." That means that on any given Sunday, anything can happen.

1869	Rutgers and Princeton play each other in the first college football games.
1891	Walter Camp, one of the primary developers of football, first publishes his book, *American Football.*
1892	William "Pudge" Heffelfinger earns $500 to play a football game. It is the first documented case of a player being paid to play football.
1901	The University of Michigan caps a perfect 11–0 season by beating Stanford in the first Rose Bowl 49–0. Michigan outscores its opponents 550–0 that season.
1906	The forward pass is legalized in college football.
1920	For the first time, professional football is organized with the formation of the APFA (later named the NFL).
1922	For the first time, a college football game—played between Chicago and Princeton—is broadcast by radio across the country.
1933	The first NFL Championship Game is played, with the Chicago Bears defeating the New York Giants.
1935	Jay Berwanger from the University of Chicago wins the first Heisman Trophy.
1936	The Associated Press poll makes its debut in college football. The University of Minnesota is the first team to be ranked number one, after starting the season 4–0. Minnesota also finishes that season at number one.
1960	The AFL is formed. The eight-team league eventually proves to be a rival of the established NFL.

1963	The Pro Football Hall of Fame opens in Canton, Ohio.
1966	The AFL and NFL agree to pit their champions against each other in a pro football title game. In January 1967, the NFL's Green Bay Packers defeat the AFL's Kansas City Chiefs in what later became known as Super Bowl I.
1970	The AFL and NFL merge into one, 26-team league. *Monday Night Football* becomes a weekly fixture in the NFL.
1973	On January 14, the Miami Dolphins defeat the Washington Redskins in Super Bowl VII to finish 17–0. Through 2011, that was the only team to ever go undefeated throughout the regular season and playoffs.
1987	For the second time in six seasons, NFL players go on strike during the season. Replacement players fill in for three weeks.
1990	Quarterback Joe Montana leads the San Francisco 49ers to their fourth Super Bowl of the decade following the 1989 season.
1991	The Associated Press names the University of Miami as national champion. It is the Hurricanes' fourth national title since 1983.
1999	The BCS is established as a way to determine a national champion in Division I college football.
2007	The University of Florida wins the first BCS Championship Game following the 2006 season, defeating Ohio State. Tom Brady and the New England Patriots win all 16 regular season games—becoming only the second team to go undefeated during the regular season—but they fall to the New York Giants in Super Bowl XLII.
2011	The Green Bay Packers defeat the Pittsburgh Steelers in Super Bowl XLV to win their 13th NFL title and fourth Super Bowl title. No team had as many NFL championships through 2011.

LEGENDS OF FOOTBALL

Sammy Baugh
quarterback/safety/kicker

Tom Brady
quarterback

Jim Brown
fullback

Dick Butkus
linebacker

Otto Graham
quarterback

Harold (Red) Grange
halfback

Joe Greene
defensive tackle

John Hannah
guard

Don Hutson
wide receiver

Deacon Jones
defensive end

Dick "Night Train" Lane
cornerback

Ray Lewis
linebacker

Bob Lilly
defensive tackle

Ronnie Lott
defensive back

John Mackey
tight end

Peyton Manning
quarterback

Joe Montana
quarterback

Anthony Munoz
offensive tackle

Bronko Nagurski
fullback

Ray Nitschke
linebacker

Jim Otto
center

Walter Payton
running back

Jerry Rice
wide receiver

Barry Sanders
running back

Deion Sanders
cornerback/wide receiver

Gale Sayers
halfback

Bruce Smith
defensive end

Emmitt Smith
running back

Lawrence Taylor
linebacker

Jim Thorpe
halfback

Johnny Unitas
quarterback

Adam Vinatieri
kicker

Reggie White
defensive end

GLOSSARY

bowl game
An end-of-season game that includes two college teams from different conferences that each won at least half of its games.

commissioner
The chief executive of a league, such as the NFL.

consecutive
Following one after the other.

draft
A system used by professional sports leagues to select new players in order to spread incoming talent among all teams.

enshrined
When a player is added to the Hall of Fame.

franchise
An entire sports organization, including the players, coaches, and staff.

fundamentals
Basic rules or laws of the game.

generate
To produce, or bring something into existence.

hall of fame
A place built to honor noteworthy achievements by athletes in their respective sports.

heritage
Something inherited from the past.

innovator
Someone who uses or invents new methods.

merge
To unite into a single body.

revenue
The amount of money that an organization has coming in.

stability
Continuing without change.

strike
A work stoppage by employees in protest of working conditions.

synonymous
When things go together or are closely associated.

Selected Bibliography

ESPN College Football Encyclopedia: The Complete History of the Game. New York: Random House Publishing Group, 2005. Print.

"History of Pro Football." *Pro Football Hall of Fame.* Pro Football Hall of Fame. 2011. Web. 29 Sept. 2011.

The Football Book: Expanded Edition. New York: Sports Illustrated Books, 2009. Print.

Further Readings

Bissinger, H. G. *Friday Night Lights: A Town, a Team, and a Dream.* New York: HarperPerennial, 1991. Print.

Fleder, Rob, ed. *The College Football Book.* New York: Sports Illustrated Books, 2008. Print.

MacCambridge, Michael. *America's Game: The Epic Story of How Pro Football Captured a Nation.* New York: Random House, 2004. Print.

Travers, Steven. *Pigskin Warriors: 140 Years of College Football's Greatest Traditions, Games, and Stars.* Lanham, MD: Taylor Trade Publishing, 2009. Print.

Web Links

To learn more about football, visit ABDO Publishing Company online at **www.abdopublishing.com**. Web sites about football are featured on our Book Links page. These links are routinely monitored and updated to provide the most current information available.

Places to Visit

College Football Hall of Fame

111 South St. Joseph St.
South Bend, IN 46601
(800) 440-FAME (3263)
www.collegefootball.org
This hall of fame and museum highlights the greatest players and moments in the history of college football. Among those enshrined are Walter Camp, Red Grange, Bo Jackson, Jim Thorpe, and Pat Tillman.

Pro Football Hall of Fame

2121 George Halas Dr., NW
Canton, OH 44708
(330) 456-8207
www.profootballhof.com
This hall of fame and museum highlights the greatest players and moments in the history of the National Football League. Jim Brown, Dick Butkus, Joe Montana, Walter Payton, and coach Vince Lombardi are among the people enshrined. A new class is enshrined prior to each NFL season. The celebration includes an NFL exhibition game.

INDEX

About the Author

Brian Howell is a freelance writer based in Colorado. He has a bachelor's degree in journalism, with a minor in history. He has had several books published about sports and history. Howell lives with his wife and four children in his native Colorado.